EMMANUEL JOSEPH

Manufacturing a New Career Narrative

Copyright © 2025 by Emmanuel Joseph

All rights reserved. No part of this publication may be reproduced, stored or transmitted in any form or by any means, electronic, mechanical, photocopying, recording, scanning, or otherwise without written permission from the publisher. It is illegal to copy this book, post it to a website, or distribute it by any other means without permission.

First edition

This book was professionally typeset on Reedsy. Find out more at reedsy.com

Contents

1	Chapter 1	1
2	Chapter 1: Discovering Your Passion	4
3	Chapter 2: Setting Clear Goals	6
4	Chapter 3: Building a Personal Brand	8
5	Chapter 4: Leveraging Your Network	10
6	Chapter 5: Gaining Relevant Experience	11
7	Chapter 6: Developing Key Skills	12
8	Chapter 7: Crafting a Compelling Resume	13
9	Chapter 8: Mastering the Job Interview	14
10	Chapter 9: Navigating Career Transitions	15
11	Chapter 10: Embracing Lifelong Learning	17
12	Chapter 11: Balancing Work and Life	19
13	Chapter 12: Sustaining Career Success	20

1

Chapter 1

Introduction

Embarking on a journey to redefine your career narrative is both exhilarating and daunting. In a world where professional paths are increasingly dynamic and multifaceted, the ability to adapt and reinvent oneself has never been more crucial. This book is designed to guide you through the process of creating a new career story that aligns with your passions, values, and aspirations. It's about taking control of your professional destiny and crafting a narrative that reflects your true self.

The modern job market is a constantly shifting landscape, influenced by technological advancements, economic changes, and evolving societal norms. Traditional career trajectories are becoming less common, and the notion of a "job for life" is increasingly rare. Instead, individuals are encouraged to pursue diverse experiences, continuously learn, and remain adaptable. This paradigm shift presents both challenges and opportunities, requiring a proactive approach to career development.

At the heart of manufacturing a new career narrative is self-discovery. Understanding who you are, what drives you, and where your strengths lie is fundamental to creating a fulfilling professional life. This involves introspection and reflection, as well as seeking feedback from others to gain a holistic view of your abilities and potential. By delving deep into your personal and professional identity, you can uncover the unique qualities that set you apart and identify the career paths that align with your core values.

Setting clear and achievable goals is the next step in this transformative process. Goals provide direction and motivation, serving as a roadmap to guide your journey. By breaking down your long-term vision into smaller, manageable objectives, you can create a structured plan that keeps you focused and accountable. This approach not only helps you track your progress but also allows for flexibility and adaptation as new opportunities and challenges arise.

Building a strong personal brand is essential in today's competitive job market. Your personal brand is the culmination of your skills, experiences, and values, and it serves as a powerful tool for communicating your professional identity to others. Developing a consistent and authentic brand message that resonates with your audience can open doors to new opportunities and set you apart from the competition. This involves leveraging online platforms, networking strategically, and continuously investing in your personal and professional growth.

Networking plays a pivotal role in manufacturing a new career narrative. Building and nurturing relationships with industry professionals, mentors, and peers can provide valuable insights, support, and opportunities. Effective networking requires a genuine approach, focusing on mutual benefit and long-term relationships rather than short-term gains. By actively engaging with your network and offering value to others, you can create a supportive community that helps you navigate the complexities of your career journey.

Gaining relevant experience is crucial for building credibility and expertise in your chosen field. This can be achieved through various means, such as internships, volunteer work, freelance projects, or lateral moves within your current organization. Hands-on experience not only enhances your skills and knowledge but also demonstrates your commitment and adaptability to potential employers. Embracing new challenges and continuously seeking opportunities for growth can accelerate your career progression and broaden your professional horizons.

Finally, maintaining a growth mindset is key to sustaining long-term career success. This involves embracing lifelong learning, staying open to new experiences, and viewing challenges as opportunities for growth. A growth mindset fosters resilience, adaptability, and a proactive approach to personal and professional development. By cultivating this mindset, you can navigate the ever-changing job market with confidence and agility, continuously evolving and thriving in your career journey.

2

Chapter 1: Discovering Your Passion

Finding your career passion is like a journey through uncharted territory. It starts with introspection, delving into what truly excites you. Many people spend years working in fields that don't align with their interests, simply because they haven't taken the time to discover what they love. Reflect on moments when you felt most alive and engaged, and consider how those moments might translate into a career.

Next, gather information about potential career paths. Research different industries, job roles, and required skills. Talk to professionals in those fields, attend workshops, and read extensively. This exploratory phase is crucial for understanding the landscape and identifying where your passions could fit.

Take a proactive approach to gaining experience. Volunteer, intern, or take on side projects to test the waters. These hands-on experiences will provide valuable insights into whether a particular field or role is a good fit for you. Additionally, they build your resume and demonstrate your commitment to potential employers.

Network with individuals who share your interests. Join professional organizations, attend industry events, and connect with people on social media platforms like LinkedIn. Building relationships within your chosen field can open doors to opportunities and provide valuable mentorship and guidance.

Finally, be patient and persistent. Discovering your true passion and aligning it with a career can take time. It's a process of trial and error, self-discovery, and continuous learning. Stay open to new experiences and be willing to adapt your plans as you gain more insights into what truly fulfills you.

3

Chapter 2: Setting Clear Goals

Once you've identified your passion, it's time to set clear career goals. Start by defining your long-term vision. Where do you see yourself in five, ten, or twenty years? Having a clear vision provides a sense of direction and purpose, guiding your decisions and actions along the way.

Break down your long-term vision into smaller, manageable goals. These short-term objectives should be specific, measurable, achievable, relevant, and time-bound (SMART). For example, if your long-term goal is to become a marketing director, a short-term goal might be to complete a marketing certification course within six months.

Create a detailed action plan for achieving your goals. Outline the steps you need to take, the resources you'll need, and any potential obstacles you might face. This plan will serve as a roadmap, helping you stay focused and organized as you work towards your objectives.

Regularly review and adjust your goals as needed. The path to success is rarely linear, and you may need to adapt your plans in response to new information or changing circumstances. Stay flexible and be willing to revise your goals if necessary to stay aligned with your evolving vision.

Celebrate your achievements along the way. Recognizing your progress and accomplishments, no matter how small, can boost your motivation and confidence. Take the time to reflect on what you've learned and how far

CHAPTER 2: SETTING CLEAR GOALS

you've come, and use that momentum to keep pushing forward.

4

Chapter 3: Building a Personal Brand

Your personal brand is the unique combination of skills, experiences, and values that define you as a professional. Start by identifying your strengths and areas of expertise. What sets you apart from others in your field? Consider the qualities that make you unique and valuable to potential employers.

Develop a consistent message that communicates your personal brand. This message should be clear, concise, and reflective of your professional identity. It should convey who you are, what you do, and what makes you different. Use this message across all your professional communication channels, including your resume, LinkedIn profile, and personal website.

Create a strong online presence to showcase your personal brand. Develop a professional LinkedIn profile that highlights your achievements, skills, and experiences. Share relevant content, engage with industry leaders, and participate in online discussions to build your reputation and credibility.

Network strategically to promote your personal brand. Attend industry events, join professional organizations, and connect with key influencers in your field. Building strong relationships with others can help you gain visibility and open doors to new opportunities.

Continuously invest in your personal and professional development. Stay up-to-date with industry trends, pursue additional education or certifications, and seek out new experiences that will enhance your skills and knowledge.

CHAPTER 3: BUILDING A PERSONAL BRAND

A strong personal brand is built on a foundation of continuous growth and improvement.

5

Chapter 4: Leveraging Your Network

Your professional network is one of your most valuable assets. Start by mapping out your existing network. Identify the people you already know, including colleagues, mentors, classmates, and industry contacts. Consider how these connections can support your career goals.

Expand your network by actively seeking out new connections. Attend industry events, join professional organizations, and participate in online communities. Be proactive in reaching out to people and building relationships. Networking is not just about meeting new people but also about nurturing and maintaining existing relationships.

Leverage your network for career opportunities. Let your connections know about your career goals and ask for their support and advice. Your network can provide valuable insights, referrals, and introductions to potential employers. Don't be afraid to ask for help when you need it.

Offer value to your network in return. Networking is a two-way street, and it's important to give as much as you receive. Share your expertise, provide support, and look for ways to help others achieve their goals. Building a strong and supportive network requires mutual trust and reciprocity.

Stay engaged with your network over time. Regularly check in with your connections, share updates on your progress, and express your gratitude for their support. Maintaining strong relationships requires ongoing effort, but the benefits are well worth it.

6

Chapter 5: Gaining Relevant Experience

Experience is key to building a successful career. Start by identifying the skills and experiences that are most relevant to your career goals. Research job descriptions and industry trends to understand what employers are looking for.

Seek out opportunities to gain relevant experience. This could include internships, part-time jobs, volunteer work, or freelance projects. Look for roles that will allow you to develop the skills and knowledge you need to advance in your career.

Take on challenging assignments that push you out of your comfort zone. These experiences can provide valuable learning opportunities and help you build resilience and adaptability. Don't be afraid to take risks and embrace new challenges.

Reflect on your experiences and what you've learned from them. Consider how each experience has contributed to your growth and development. Use these insights to refine your career goals and identify areas for further improvement.

Document your experiences and achievements. Keep a record of your accomplishments, including specific examples of projects you've worked on, skills you've developed, and results you've achieved. This documentation will be valuable when updating your resume and preparing for job interviews.

7

Chapter 6: Developing Key Skills

Skills are the building blocks of a successful career. Start by identifying the key skills that are essential for your chosen field. Research industry standards and job descriptions to understand the skills that are in high demand.

Invest in your education and professional development. Take courses, attend workshops, and pursue certifications to build your skills and knowledge. Look for opportunities to learn from experts in your field and stay up-to-date with the latest industry trends.

Practice and apply your skills in real-world situations. Look for opportunities to use your skills on the job, in volunteer roles, or through side projects. The more you practice, the more proficient and confident you will become.

Seek feedback from others to improve your skills. Ask for constructive criticism from colleagues, mentors, and supervisors. Use their feedback to identify areas for improvement and develop a plan for addressing them.

Continuously assess and update your skills. The job market is constantly evolving, and it's important to stay current with the latest developments in your field. Regularly review your skills and identify any gaps that need to be addressed. Stay proactive in seeking out new learning opportunities.

8

Chapter 7: Crafting a Compelling Resume

Your resume is your marketing tool. Start by creating a clear and concise resume that highlights your key achievements and experiences. Focus on the skills and accomplishments that are most relevant to the job you're applying for.

Use a clean and professional format that is easy to read. Avoid clutter and unnecessary information. Use bullet points to break up text and make it easier for hiring managers to quickly scan your resume.

Tailor your resume to each job application. Customize your resume to match the job description and emphasize the skills and experiences that are most relevant to the position. Use keywords from the job description to increase your chances of getting noticed by applicant tracking systems.

Highlight your achievements and quantify your results. Use specific examples and metrics to demonstrate the impact of your work. This will help you stand out from other candidates and show potential employers what you can bring to the table.

Proofread your resume carefully to avoid any errors or typos. A polished and error-free resume reflects your attention to detail and professionalism. Consider asking a trusted friend or mentor to review your resume and provide feedback.

9

Chapter 8: Mastering the Job Interview

Preparing for a job interview is crucial for success. Start by researching the company and the role you're applying for. Understand their mission, values, and culture, and be ready to explain how you align with them.

Practice common interview questions and develop strong responses. Prepare examples that demonstrate your skills, experiences, and achievements. Use the STAR method (Situation, Task, Action, Result) to structure your answers and provide clear and concise responses.

Dress professionally and arrive on time for the interview. First impressions matter, and dressing appropriately shows that you take the opportunity seriously. Arriving on time demonstrates your punctuality and respect for the interviewer's time.

During the interview, be confident and enthusiastic. Show your interest in the role and the company by asking thoughtful questions and engaging in the conversation. Listen carefully to the interviewer's questions and take your time to provide well-thought-out answers.

Follow up after the interview with a thank-you note. Express your gratitude for the opportunity and reiterate your interest in the position. A thoughtful thank-you note can leave a positive impression and help you stand out from other candidates.

10

Chapter 9: Navigating Career Transitions

Career transitions can be challenging but also offer new opportunities for growth and reinvention. Start by acknowledging the reasons for your transition. Whether it's due to layoffs, a desire for change, or personal circumstances, understanding the motivations behind your transition can help you navigate it more effectively.

Take time to assess your current skills and experiences. Identify the transferable skills that can be applied to your new career path. Consider taking additional courses or gaining certifications to fill any gaps in your knowledge.

Seek support from your network. Reach out to mentors, colleagues, and industry contacts for advice and guidance. Their insights can provide valuable perspectives and help you identify potential opportunities. Networking can also lead to referrals and introductions to potential employers.

Stay open to new experiences and be willing to step out of your comfort zone. Career transitions often involve taking risks and embracing uncertainty. Be proactive in seeking out new opportunities and be flexible in adapting to changing circumstances.

Maintain a positive mindset and stay resilient. Career transitions can be stressful, and it's important to stay focused on your goals. Celebrate small wins along the way and remind yourself of your progress. Staying positive and persistent will help you navigate the challenges and make the most of new opportunities.

11

Chapter 10: Embracing Lifelong Learning

In today's rapidly changing job market, lifelong learning is essential for career success. Stay curious and open to new experiences. Continuously seek out opportunities to learn and grow, both personally and professionally.

Invest in your education and professional development. Take advantage of online courses, workshops, and seminars to build new skills and stay up-to-date with industry trends. Consider pursuing advanced degrees or certifications to enhance your knowledge and credentials.

Engage in self-directed learning. Read books, listen to podcasts, and watch educational videos to expand your knowledge. Join professional organizations and participate in industry events to stay connected with the latest developments in your field.

Reflect on your learning experiences and apply what you've learned to your career. Consider how new knowledge and skills can be used to solve problems, improve processes, and drive innovation. Lifelong learning is not just about acquiring new information, but also about applying it in meaningful ways.

Foster a growth mindset and embrace challenges as opportunities for learning. Recognize that setbacks and failures are part of the learning process. Use them as opportunities to reflect, learn, and grow. A commitment to lifelong learning will help you stay adaptable and resilient in an ever-changing job market.

12

Chapter 11: Balancing Work and Life

Achieving a healthy work-life balance is essential for long-term career satisfaction. Start by setting clear boundaries between work and personal life. Establish specific times for work and leisure, and stick to them as much as possible.

Prioritize self-care and make time for activities that bring you joy and relaxation. Engage in hobbies, exercise regularly, and spend time with loved ones. Taking care of your physical and mental well-being is crucial for maintaining productivity and avoiding burnout.

Develop effective time management skills. Plan your day and prioritize tasks to ensure that you stay focused and organized. Use tools and techniques, such as to-do lists, calendars, and time-blocking, to manage your time effectively.

Communicate your needs and boundaries with your employer and colleagues. Be open and honest about your availability and workload. Setting realistic expectations and managing communication can help reduce stress and improve work-life balance.

Regularly assess and adjust your work-life balance as needed. Life circumstances and work demands can change over time, and it's important to stay flexible and adapt to new challenges. Continuously strive to find a balance that works for you and supports your overall well-being.

13

Chapter 12: Sustaining Career Success

Sustaining career success requires ongoing effort and dedication. Stay proactive in seeking out new opportunities for growth and advancement. Continuously set new goals and challenge yourself to reach higher levels of achievement.

Build a strong professional reputation by consistently delivering high-quality work and demonstrating integrity and reliability. Develop strong relationships with colleagues, mentors, and industry leaders who can support your career growth.

Stay adaptable and open to change. The job market and industry trends are constantly evolving, and it's important to stay flexible and responsive to new opportunities and challenges. Embrace a mindset of continuous improvement and be willing to adapt your plans as needed.

Seek feedback and continuously evaluate your performance. Regularly assess your progress towards your goals and identify areas for improvement. Use feedback from others to refine your skills and strategies.

Maintain a positive attitude and stay motivated. Celebrate your achievements and stay focused on your long-term vision. Sustaining career success requires perseverance, resilience, and a commitment to continuous growth and development.

Book Description: Manufacturing a New Career Narrative

In an ever-evolving job market, where traditional career paths are becoming less common, the ability to adapt and reinvent oneself has never been more important. "Manufacturing a New Career Narrative" is your ultimate guide to taking control of your professional destiny and crafting a career that truly reflects your passions, values, and aspirations.

This comprehensive book takes you on a transformative journey of self-discovery, goal-setting, and personal branding. It begins with an exploration of your unique strengths and interests, helping you uncover the career paths that align with your true self. Through practical advice and actionable steps, you'll learn how to set clear, achievable goals and develop a strategic plan to reach them.

You'll discover the importance of building a strong personal brand and how to effectively communicate your professional identity to stand out in a competitive job market. The book delves into the power of networking, offering insights on how to build and leverage meaningful connections that can open doors to new opportunities.

Gaining relevant experience and continuously developing key skills are crucial components of career success. This book provides guidance on how to seek out hands-on experiences, embrace new challenges, and stay current with industry trends. It emphasizes the importance of lifelong learning and maintaining a growth mindset to navigate the ever-changing job landscape with confidence and agility.

Balancing work and life is another essential aspect covered in this book. You'll learn strategies for setting boundaries, managing your time effectively, and prioritizing self-care to achieve a healthy work-life balance. The book also addresses the challenges and opportunities of career transitions, offering practical advice on how to navigate these changes and emerge stronger and more fulfilled.

"Manufacturing a New Career Narrative" is not just about achieving short-term success; it's about sustaining long-term career satisfaction. The book emphasizes the importance of continuous growth, resilience, and adaptability, providing you with the tools and mindset needed to thrive in your professional journey.

Whether you're at the beginning of your career, seeking a mid-career change, or looking to enhance your current path, this book will inspire and guide you to create a career narrative that is uniquely yours. Join the journey and unlock the potential for a fulfilling and successful career.

www.ingramcontent.com/pod-product-compliance
Lightning Source LLC
LaVergne TN
LVHW020508080526
838202LV00057B/6236